"Family Financial Planner" by Adeola Ayanwale.

The copyright and the rights of translation in any language are reserved by the publishers and copyright owner. No part, passage, text or photograph, or artwork of this book should be reproduced, transmitted, or utilized (except for short passages for the purposes of review and publicity), in the original language or by translation, in any form or by any means, electronic, mechanical, photocopying, recording by any information storage and retrieval system except with the express and prior permission, in writing, from the copyright author.

Copyright © 2021 by Adeola Ayanwale.

Produced by Lavade groups Ltd Co. Published in the USA through Amazon KDP.

MY LONG-TERM GOALS

Something that will take you a long time to accomplish.

FINANCIAL

HEALTH

LEGACY

RELATIONSHIP

CAREER/PERSONAL DEVELOPMENT

SHORT-TERM GOALS

What is a short-term goal?

A short-term goal is something you want to do in the near future. The near future can mean today, this week, or this month. A short-term goal is something you want to accomplish soon.

Financial	Health	Personal Development

Action Steps:

- ○ _____
- ○ _____
- ○ _____
- ○ _____

Action Steps:

- ○ _____
- ○ _____
- ○ _____
- ○ _____

Action Steps:

- ○ _____
- ○ _____
- ○ _____
- ○ _____

January
2022

S	M	T	W	T	F	S
						1
2	3	4	5	6	7	8
9	10	11	12	13	14	15
16	17	18	19	20	21	22
23	24	25	26	27	28	29
30	31					

Weekly Schedule Planner

Week No. _____

THIS WEEK'S GOALS

TO-DO CHECKLIST

NOTES/REMINDERS

"A BUDGET DOESN'T LIMIT YOUR FREEDOM; IT GIVES YOU FREEDOM."

HABIT TRACKER

Week: _____

ACTIVITIES	M	T	W	T	F	S	S

NOTES

Weekly Schedule Planner

Week No. _____

THIS WEEK'S GOALS

TO-DO CHECKLIST

NOTES/REMINDERS

"THE POOR AND THE MIDDLE-CLASS WORK FOR MONEY. THE RICH HAVE MONEY WORK FOR THEM."

HABIT TRACKER

Week: _____

ACTIVITIES	M	T	W	T	F	S	S

NOTES

Weekly Schedule Planner

Week No. _____

THIS WEEK'S GOALS

TO-DO CHECKLIST

NOTES/REMINDERS

"COMPOUND INTEREST IS THE EIGHTH WONDER OF THE WORLD. HE WHO UNDERSTANDS IT, EARNS IT. HE WHO DOESN'T, PAYS IT."

HABIT TRACKER

Week: _____

ACTIVITIES	M	T	W	T	F	S	S

NOTES

Weekly Schedule Planner

Week No. _____

THIS WEEK'S GOALS

TO-DO CHECKLIST

NOTES/REMINDERS

"THE BEST TIME TO PLANT A TREE IS 20 YEARS AGO. THE SECOND BEST TIME IS NOW."

HABIT TRACKER

Week: _____

ACTIVITIES	M	T	W	T	F	S	S

NOTES

MONTHLY BUDGET

Month :

ITEM	BUDGET	SPENT	REMAINS

TOTAL:

Notes

GIFT PLANNING

DATE:

GIFTS TO BE GIVEN	BUDGET	ACTUAL	
			✓
			☐
			☐
			☐
			☐
			☐
			☐
			☐
			☐

NOTES:

MY TRAVEL PLAN

Date: _____

Date:

Location:

Budget:

Travel To-do List

-
-
-
-
-
-
-

Today's Expenses

Today's Log

6 AM	
7 AM	
8 AM	
9 AM	
10 AM	
11 AM	
12 PM	
1 PM	
2 PM	
3 PM	
4 PM	
5 PM	
6 PM	
7 PM	
8 PM	

Quick Note:

GOALS ACHIEVED THIS MONTH!

Goals: Checklist

- [ ]
- [ ]
- [ ]
- [ ]
- [ ]
- [ ]
- [ ]
- [ ]

February
2022

S	M	T	W	T	F	S
		1	2	3	4	5
6	7	8	9	10	11	12
13	14	15	16	17	18	19
20	21	22	23	24	25	26
27	28					

Weekly Schedule Planner

Week No. _____

THIS WEEK'S GOALS

TO-DO CHECKLIST

NOTES/REMINDERS

"TRUE WEALTH IS NOT OF THE POCKET, BUT OF THE HEART AND MIND."

HABIT TRACKER

Week: _____

ACTIVITIES	M	T	W	T	F	S	S

NOTES

Weekly Schedule Planner

Week No. _____

THIS WEEK'S GOALS

TO-DO CHECKLIST

NOTES/REMINDERS

"WEALTH FLOWS FROM ENERGY AND IDEAS."

HABIT TRACKER

Week: _____

ACTIVITIES	M	T	W	T	F	S	S

NOTES

Weekly Schedule Planner

Week No. _____

THIS WEEK'S GOALS

TO-DO CHECKLIST

NOTES/REMINDERS

"WEALTH IS JUST CONSISTENCY... I DON'T WANT TO BE RICH, I WANT TO BE WEALTHY."

HABIT TRACKER

Week: _____

ACTIVITIES	M	T	W	T	F	S	S

NOTES

Weekly Schedule Planner

Week No. _____

THIS WEEK'S GOALS

TO-DO CHECKLIST

NOTES/REMINDERS

"THE GREATEST WEALTH IS TO LIVE CONTENT WITH LITTLE."

HABIT TRACKER

Week: _____

ACTIVITIES	M	T	W	T	F	S	S

NOTES

MONTHLY BUDGET

Month :

ITEM	BUDGET	SPENT	REMAINS

TOTAL:

Notes

GIFT PLANNING

DATE:

GIFTS TO BE GIVEN	BUDGET	ACTUAL	
			✓
			☐
			☐
			☐
			☐
			☐
			☐
			☐
			☐

NOTES:

MY TRAVEL PLAN

Date: _____

Date:

Location:

Budget:

Travel To-do List

Today's Expenses

Today's Log

- 6 AM
- 7 AM
- 8 AM
- 9 AM
- 10 AM
- 11 AM
- 12 PM
- 1 PM
- 2 PM
- 3 PM
- 4 PM
- 5 PM
- 6 PM
- 7 PM
- 8 PM

Quick Note:

GOALS ACHIEVED THIS MONTH!

Goals: Checklist

☐
☐
☐
☐
☐
☐
☐
☐

March

2022

S	M	T	W	T	F	S
		1	2	3	4	5
6	7	8	9	10	11	12
13	14	15	16	17	18	19
20	21	22	23	24	25	26
27	28	29	30	31		

Weekly Schedule Planner

Week No. _____

THIS WEEK'S GOALS

TO-DO CHECKLIST

NOTES/REMINDERS

"IT IS GREAT WEALTH TO A SOUL TO LIVE FRUGALLY WITH A CONTENTED MIND."

HABIT TRACKER

Week: _____

ACTIVITIES	M	T	W	T	F	S	S

NOTES

Weekly Schedule Planner

Week No. _____

THIS WEEK'S GOALS

TO-DO CHECKLIST

NOTES/REMINDERS

"DO NOT SAVE WHAT IS LEFT AFTER SPENDING, BUT SPEND WHAT IS LEFT AFTER SAVING."

HABIT TRACKER

Week: _____

ACTIVITIES	M	T	W	T	F	S	S

NOTES

Weekly Schedule Planner

Week No. _____

THIS WEEK'S GOALS

TO-DO CHECKLIST

NOTES/REMINDERS

"YOU MUST GAIN CONTROL OVER YOUR MONEY OR THE LACK OF IT WILL FOREVER CONTROL YOU."

HABIT TRACKER

Week: _____

ACTIVITIES	M	T	W	T	F	S	S

NOTES

Weekly Schedule Planner

Week No. _____

THIS WEEK'S GOALS

TO-DO CHECKLIST

NOTES/REMINDERS

"A MAN WHO BOTH SPENDS AND SAVES MONEY IS THE HAPPIEST MAN, BECAUSE HE HAS BOTH ENJOYMENTS."

HABIT TRACKER

Week: _____

ACTIVITIES	M	T	W	T	F	S	S

NOTES

MONTHLY BUDGET

Month :

ITEM	BUDGET	SPENT	REMAINS

TOTAL:

Notes

GIFT PLANNING

DATE:

GIFTS TO BE GIVEN	BUDGET	ACTUAL	
			✓
			☐
			☐
			☐
			☐
			☐
			☐
			☐
			☐

NOTES:

MY TRAVEL PLAN

Date: _____

| Date: | Today's Log |

Location:

Budget:

Travel To-do List

- 6 AM
- 7 AM
- 8 AM
- 9 AM
- 10 AM
- 11 AM
- 12 PM
- 1 PM
- 2 PM
- 3 PM
- 4 PM
- 5 PM
- 6 PM
- 7 PM
- 8 PM

Today's Expenses

Quick Note:

GOALS ACHIEVED THIS MONTH!

Goals: Checklist

- [ ]
- [ ]
- [ ]
- [ ]
- [ ]
- [ ]
- [ ]
- [ ]

April
2022

S	M	T	W	T	F	S
					1	2
3	4	5	6	7	8	9
10	11	12	13	14	15	16
17	18	19	20	21	22	23
24	25	26	27	28	29	30

Weekly Schedule Planner

Week No. _____

THIS WEEK'S GOALS

TO-DO CHECKLIST

NOTES/REMINDERS

"YOU DON'T HAVE TO SEE THE WHOLE STAIRCASE, JUST TAKE THE FIRST STEP."

HABIT TRACKER

Week: _____

ACTIVITIES	M	T	W	T	F	S	S

NOTES

Weekly Schedule Planner

Week No. _____

THIS WEEK'S GOALS

TO-DO CHECKLIST

NOTES/REMINDERS

"EMPTY POCKETS NEVER HELD ANYONE BACK. ONLY EMPTY HEADS AND EMPTY HEARTS CAN DO THAT."

HABIT TRACKER

Week: _____

ACTIVITIES	M	T	W	T	F	S	S

NOTES

Weekly Schedule Planner

Week No. _____

THIS WEEK'S GOALS

TO-DO CHECKLIST

NOTES/REMINDERS

"IT IS THRIFTY TO PREPARE TODAY FOR THE WANTS OF TOMORROW."

HABIT TRACKER

Week: _____

ACTIVITIES	M	T	W	T	F	S	S

NOTES

Weekly Schedule Planner

Week No. _____

THIS WEEK'S GOALS

TO-DO CHECKLIST

NOTES/REMINDERS

"MONEY AMASSED EITHER SERVES US OR RULES US."

HABIT TRACKER

Week: _____

ACTIVITIES	M	T	W	T	F	S	S

NOTES

MONTHLY BUDGET

Month :

ITEM	BUDGET	SPENT	REMAINS

TOTAL:

Notes

GIFT PLANNING

DATE:

GIFTS TO BE GIVEN	BUDGET	ACTUAL	✓
			☐
			☐
			☐
			☐
			☐
			☐
			☐
			☐

NOTES:

MY TRAVEL PLAN

Date: _____

Date:

Location:

Budget:

Travel To-do List

-
-
-
-
-
-
-

Today's Expenses

Today's Log

6 AM	
7 AM	
8 AM	
9 AM	
10 AM	
11 AM	
12 PM	
1 PM	
2 PM	
3 PM	
4 PM	
5 PM	
6 PM	
7 PM	
8 PM	

Quick Note:

GOALS ACHIEVED THIS MONTH!

Goals: Checklist

- [ ]
- [ ]
- [ ]
- [ ]
- [ ]
- [ ]
- [ ]
- [ ]

May
2022

S	M	T	W	T	F	S
1	2	3	4	5	6	7
8	9	10	11	12	13	14
15	16	17	18	19	20	21
22	23	24	25	26	27	28
29	30	31				

Weekly Schedule Planner

Week No. _____

THIS WEEK'S GOALS

TO-DO CHECKLIST

NOTES/REMINDERS

"HE WHO WILL NOT ECONOMIZE WILL HAVE TO AGONIZE."

HABIT TRACKER

Week: _____

ACTIVITIES	M	T	W	T	F	S	S

NOTES

Weekly Schedule Planner

Week No. _____

THIS WEEK'S GOALS

TO-DO CHECKLIST

NOTES/REMINDERS

"SMALL AMOUNTS SAVED DAILY ADD UP TO HUGE INVESTMENTS IN THE END."

HABIT TRACKER

Week: _____

ACTIVITIES	M	T	W	T	F	S	S

NOTES

Weekly Schedule Planner

Week No. _____

THIS WEEK'S GOALS

TO-DO CHECKLIST

NOTES/REMINDERS

"HE WHO BUYS WHAT HE DOES NOT NEED, STEALS FROM HIMSELF."

HABIT TRACKER

Week: _____

ACTIVITIES	M	T	W	T	F	S	S

NOTES

Weekly Schedule Planner

Week No. _____

THIS WEEK'S GOALS

TO-DO CHECKLIST

NOTES/REMINDERS

"RICH PEOPLE STAY RICH BY LIVING LIKE THEY'RE BROKE. BROKE PEOPLE STAY BROKE BY LIVING LIKE THEY'RE RICH."

HABIT TRACKER

Week: _____

ACTIVITIES	M	T	W	T	F	S	S

NOTES

MONTHLY BUDGET

Month :

ITEM	BUDGET	SPENT	REMAINS

TOTAL:

Notes

GIFT PLANNING

DATE:

GIFTS TO BE GIVEN	BUDGET	ACTUAL	✓
			☐
			☐
			☐
			☐
			☐
			☐
			☐
			☐

NOTES:

MY TRAVEL PLAN

Date: _____

Date:

Location:

Budget:

Travel To-do List

-
-
-
-
-
-
-

Today's Expenses

Today's Log

- 6 AM
- 7 AM
- 8 AM
- 9 AM
- 10 AM
- 11 AM
- 12 PM
- 1 PM
- 2 PM
- 3 PM
- 4 PM
- 5 PM
- 6 PM
- 7 PM
- 8 PM

Quick Note:

GOALS ACHIEVED THIS MONTH!

Goals: Checklist

☐
☐
☐
☐
☐
☐
☐
☐

June
2022

S	M	T	W	T	F	S
			1	2	3	4
5	6	7	8	9	10	11
12	13	14	15	16	17	18
19	20	21	22	23	24	25
26	27	28	29	30		

Half Year At Glance

JANUARY	FEBRUARY
MARCH	APRIL
MAY	JUNE

NOTES

Weekly Schedule Planner

Week No. _____

THIS WEEK'S GOALS

TO-DO CHECKLIST

NOTES/REMINDERS

"IF YOU'RE SAVING, YOU'RE SUCCEEDING."

HABIT TRACKER

Week: _____

ACTIVITIES	M	T	W	T	F	S	S

NOTES

Weekly Schedule Planner

Week No. _____

THIS WEEK'S GOALS

TO-DO CHECKLIST

NOTES/REMINDERS

"KNOW WHAT YOU OWN, AND KNOW WHY YOU OWN IT."

HABIT TRACKER

Week: _____

ACTIVITIES	M	T	W	T	F	S	S

NOTES

Weekly Schedule Planner

Week No. _____

THIS WEEK'S GOALS

TO-DO CHECKLIST

NOTES/REMINDERS

"EVERY TIME YOU BORROW MONEY, YOU'RE ROBBING YOUR FUTURE SELF."

HABIT TRACKER

Week: _____

ACTIVITIES	M	T	W	T	F	S	S

NOTES

Weekly Schedule Planner

Week No. _____

THIS WEEK'S GOALS

TO-DO CHECKLIST

NOTES/REMINDERS

"THE MORE YOU LEARN, THE MORE YOU EARN."

HABIT TRACKER

Week: _____

ACTIVITIES	M	T	W	T	F	S	S

NOTES

MONTHLY BUDGET

Month :

ITEM	BUDGET	SPENT	REMAINS

TOTAL:

Notes

GIFT PLANNING

DATE:

GIFTS TO BE GIVEN	BUDGET	ACTUAL	✓

NOTES:

MY TRAVEL PLAN

Date: _____

Date:

Location:

Budget:

Travel To-do List

Today's Log

- 6 AM
- 7 AM
- 8 AM
- 9 AM
- 10 AM
- 11 AM
- 12 PM
- 1 PM
- 2 PM
- 3 PM
- 4 PM
- 5 PM
- 6 PM
- 7 PM
- 8 PM

Today's Expenses

Quick Note:

GOALS ACHIEVED THIS MONTH!

Goals: Checklist

☐
☐
☐
☐
☐
☐
☐
☐

July
2022

S	M	T	W	T	F	S
					1	2
3	4	5	6	7	8	9
10	11	12	13	14	15	16
17	18	19	20	21	22	23
24	25	26	27	28	29	30
31						

Weekly Schedule Planner

Week No. _____

THIS WEEK'S GOALS

TO-DO CHECKLIST

NOTES/REMINDERS

"FRIENDSHIP IS LIKE MONEY, EASIER MADE THAN KEPT."

HABIT TRACKER

Week: _____

ACTIVITIES	M	T	W	T	F	S	S

NOTES

Weekly Schedule Planner

Week No. _____

THIS WEEK'S GOALS

TO-DO CHECKLIST

NOTES/REMINDERS

"MANY FOLKS THINK THEY AREN'T GOOD AT EARNING MONEY WHEN WHAT THEY DON'T KNOW IS HOW TO USE IT."

HABIT TRACKER

Week: _____

ACTIVITIES	M	T	W	T	F	S	S

NOTES

Weekly Schedule Planner

Week No. _____

THIS WEEK'S GOALS

TO-DO CHECKLIST

NOTES/REMINDERS

"MONEY GROWS ON THE TREE OF PERSISTENCE."

HABIT TRACKER

Week: _____

ACTIVITIES	M	T	W	T	F	S	S

NOTES

Weekly Schedule Planner

Week No. _____

THIS WEEK'S GOALS

TO-DO CHECKLIST

NOTES/REMINDERS

"IT TAKES AS MUCH ENERGY TO WISH AS IT DOES TO PLAN."

HABIT TRACKER

Week: _____

ACTIVITIES	M	T	W	T	F	S	S

NOTES

MONTHLY BUDGET

Month :

ITEM	BUDGET	SPENT	REMAINS

TOTAL:

Notes

GIFT PLANNING

DATE:

GIFTS TO BE GIVEN	BUDGET	ACTUAL	✓
			☐
			☐
			☐
			☐
			☐
			☐
			☐
			☐
			☐

NOTES:

MY TRAVEL PLAN

Date: _____

Date:

Location:

Budget:

Travel To-do List

-
-
-
-
-
-
-

Today's Expenses

Today's Log

6 AM	
7 AM	
8 AM	
9 AM	
10 AM	
11 AM	
12 PM	
1 PM	
2 PM	
3 PM	
4 PM	
5 PM	
6 PM	
7 PM	
8 PM	

Quick Note:

GOALS ACHIEVED THIS MONTH!

Goals: Checklist

	☐
	☐
	☐
	☐
	☐
	☐
	☐
	☐

August
2022

S	M	T	W	T	F	S
	1	2	3	4	5	6
7	8	9	10	11	12	13
14	15	16	17	18	19	20
21	22	23	24	25	26	27
28	29	30	31			

Weekly Schedule Planner

Week No. _____

THIS WEEK'S GOALS

TO-DO CHECKLIST

NOTES/REMINDERS

"MONEY IS POWER, FREEDOM, A CUSHION, THE ROOT OF ALL EVIL, THE SUM OF BLESSINGS."

HABIT TRACKER

Week: _____

ACTIVITIES	M	T	W	T	F	S	S

NOTES

Weekly Schedule Planner

Week No. _____

THIS WEEK'S GOALS

TO-DO CHECKLIST

NOTES/REMINDERS

"WEALTH IS NOT ABOUT HAVING A LOT OF MONEY; IT'S ABOUT HAVING A LOT OF OPTIONS."

HABIT TRACKER

Week: _____

ACTIVITIES	M	T	W	T	F	S	S

NOTES

Weekly Schedule Planner

Week No. _____

THIS WEEK'S GOALS

TO-DO CHECKLIST

NOTES/REMINDERS

"MONEY IS LIKE MUCK—NOT GOOD UNLESS IT IS SPREAD."

HABIT TRACKER

Week: _____

ACTIVITIES	M	T	W	T	F	S	S

NOTES

Weekly Schedule Planner

Week No. _____

THIS WEEK'S GOALS

TO-DO CHECKLIST

NOTES/REMINDERS

"YOU CAN BE YOUNG WITHOUT MONEY, BUT YOU CAN'T BE OLD WITHOUT IT."

HABIT TRACKER

Week: _____

ACTIVITIES	M	T	W	T	F	S	S

NOTES

MONTHLY BUDGET

Month :

ITEM	BUDGET	SPENT	REMAINS

TOTAL:

Notes

GIFT PLANNING

DATE:

GIFTS TO BE GIVEN	BUDGET	ACTUAL	
			✓
			☐
			☐
			☐
			☐
			☐
			☐
			☐
			☐

NOTES:

MY TRAVEL PLAN

Date: _____

Date:

Location:

Budget:

Travel To-do List

Today's Expenses

Today's Log

- 6 AM
- 7 AM
- 8 AM
- 9 AM
- 10 AM
- 11 AM
- 12 PM
- 1 PM
- 2 PM
- 3 PM
- 4 PM
- 5 PM
- 6 PM
- 7 PM
- 8 PM

Quick Note:

GOALS ACHIEVED THIS MONTH!

Goals: Checklist

	☐
	☐
	☐
	☐
	☐
	☐
	☐
	☐

September
2022

S	M	T	W	T	F	S
				1	2	3
4	5	6	7	8	9	10
11	12	13	14	15	16	17
16	19	20	21	22	23	22
25	26	27	28	29	30	

Weekly Schedule Planner

Week No. _____

THIS WEEK'S GOALS

TO-DO CHECKLIST

NOTES/REMINDERS

"THERE ARE ONLY TWO PATHS TO HAPPINESS IN LIFE. UTTER STUPIDITY OR EXCEPTIONAL WEALTH."

HABIT TRACKER

Week: _____

ACTIVITIES	M	T	W	T	F	S	S

NOTES

Weekly Schedule Planner

Week No. _____

THIS WEEK'S GOALS

TO-DO CHECKLIST

NOTES/REMINDERS

"WEALTH IS THE ABILITY TO FULLY EXPERIENCE LIFE."

HABIT TRACKER

Week: _____

ACTIVITIES	M	T	W	T	F	S	S

NOTES

Weekly Schedule Planner

Week No. _____

THIS WEEK'S GOALS

TO-DO CHECKLIST

NOTES/REMINDERS

"We make a living by what we get, but we make a life by what we give."

HABIT TRACKER

Week: _____

ACTIVITIES	M	T	W	T	F	S	S

NOTES

Weekly Schedule Planner

Week No. _____

THIS WEEK'S GOALS

TO-DO CHECKLIST

NOTES/REMINDERS

"BUDGETING HAS ONLY ONE RULE: DO NOT GO OVER BUDGET."

HABIT TRACKER

Week: _____

ACTIVITIES	M	T	W	T	F	S	S

NOTES

MONTHLY BUDGET

Month :

ITEM	BUDGET	SPENT	REMAINS

TOTAL:

Notes

GIFT PLANNING

DATE:

GIFTS TO BE GIVEN	BUDGET	ACTUAL	✓
			☐
			☐
			☐
			☐
			☐
			☐
			☐
			☐
			☐

NOTES:

MY TRAVEL PLAN

Date: _____

Date:

Location:

Budget:

Travel To-do List

-
-
-
-
-
-

Today's Expenses

Today's Log

- 6 AM
- 7 AM
- 8 AM
- 9 AM
- 10 AM
- 11 AM
- 12 PM
- 1 PM
- 2 PM
- 3 PM
- 4 PM
- 5 PM
- 6 PM
- 7 PM
- 8 PM

Quick Note:

GOALS ACHIEVED THIS MONTH!

Goals: Checklist

	☐
	☐
	☐
	☐
	☐
	☐
	☐
	☐

October
2022

S	M	T	W	T	F	S
						1
2	3	4	5	6	7	8
9	10	11	12	13	14	15
16	17	18	19	20	21	22
23	24	25	26	27	28	29
30	31					

Weekly Schedule Planner

Week No. _____

THIS WEEK'S GOALS

TO-DO CHECKLIST

NOTES/REMINDERS

"THE SECRET TO BUDGETING IS THAT IT NEEDS TO BE HONEST."

HABIT TRACKER

Week: _____

ACTIVITIES	M	T	W	T	F	S	S

NOTES

Weekly Schedule Planner

Week No. _____

THIS WEEK'S GOALS

TO-DO CHECKLIST

NOTES/REMINDERS

"THE SECRET TO BUDGETING IS THAT IT NEEDS TO BE HONEST."

HABIT TRACKER

Week: _____

ACTIVITIES	M	T	W	T	F	S	S

NOTES

Weekly Schedule Planner

Week No. _____

THIS WEEK'S GOALS

TO-DO CHECKLIST

NOTES/REMINDERS

"IF YOU DON'T GET SERIOUS ABOUT YOUR MONEY, YOU WILL NEVER HAVE SERIOUS MONEY."

HABIT TRACKER

Week: _____

ACTIVITIES	M	T	W	T	F	S	S

NOTES

Weekly Schedule Planner

Week No. _____

THIS WEEK'S GOALS

TO-DO CHECKLIST

NOTES/REMINDERS

"MONEY, LIKE EMOTIONS, IS SOMETHING YOU MUST CONTROL TO KEEP YOUR LIFE ON THE RIGHT TRACK."

HABIT TRACKER

Week: _____

ACTIVITIES	M	T	W	T	F	S	S

NOTES

MONTHLY BUDGET

Month :

ITEM	BUDGET	SPENT	REMAINS

TOTAL:

Notes

GIFT PLANNING

DATE:

GIFTS TO BE GIVEN	BUDGET	ACTUAL	✓
			☐
			☐
			☐
			☐
			☐
			☐
			☐
			☐
			☐

NOTES:

MY TRAVEL PLAN

Date: _____

Date:

Location:

Budget:

Travel To-do List

-
-
-
-
-
-
-

Today's Expenses

Today's Log

6 AM	
7 AM	
8 AM	
9 AM	
10 AM	
11 AM	
12 PM	
1 PM	
2 PM	
3 PM	
4 PM	
5 PM	
6 PM	
7 PM	
8 PM	

Quick Note:

GOALS ACHIEVED THIS MONTH!

Goals: Checklist

☐
☐
☐
☐
☐
☐
☐
☐

November

2022

S	M	T	W	T	F	S
		1	2	3	4	5
6	7	8	9	10	11	12
13	14	15	16	17	18	19
20	21	22	23	24	25	26
27	28	29	30			

Weekly Schedule Planner

Week No. _____

THIS WEEK'S GOALS

TO-DO CHECKLIST

NOTES/REMINDERS

"THE GREATEST WEALTH IS TO LIVE CONTENT WITH LITTLE."

HABIT TRACKER

Week: _____

ACTIVITIES	M	T	W	T	F	S	S

NOTES

Weekly Schedule Planner

Week No. _____

THIS WEEK'S GOALS

TO-DO CHECKLIST

NOTES/REMINDERS

"EVERY CENT YOU OWN AND EVERY MOMENT YOU SPEND IS ALWAYS AN INVESTMENT."

HABIT TRACKER

Week: _____

ACTIVITIES	M	T	W	T	F	S	S

NOTES

Weekly Schedule Planner

Week No. _____

THIS WEEK'S GOALS

TO-DO CHECKLIST

NOTES/REMINDERS

"THOSE WHO DON'T MANAGE THEIR MONEY WILL ALWAYS WORK FOR THOSE WHO DO."

HABIT TRACKER

Week: _____

ACTIVITIES	M	T	W	T	F	S	S

NOTES

Weekly Schedule Planner

Week No. _____

THIS WEEK'S GOALS

TO-DO CHECKLIST

NOTES/REMINDERS

"THE SLIGHTEST ADJUSTMENTS TO YOUR DAILY ROUTINES CAN DRAMATICALLY ALTER THE OUTCOMES IN YOUR LIFE."

HABIT TRACKER

Week: _____

ACTIVITIES	M	T	W	T	F	S	S

NOTES

MONTHLY BUDGET

Month :

ITEM	BUDGET	SPENT	REMAINS

TOTAL:

Notes

GIFT PLANNING

DATE:

GIFTS TO BE GIVEN	BUDGET	ACTUAL	✓

NOTES:

MY TRAVEL PLAN

Date: _____

Date:

Location:

Budget:

Travel To-do List

Today's Expenses

Today's Log

- 6 AM
- 7 AM
- 8 AM
- 9 AM
- 10 AM
- 11 AM
- 12 PM
- 1 PM
- 2 PM
- 3 PM
- 4 PM
- 5 PM
- 6 PM
- 7 PM
- 8 PM

Quick Note:

GOALS ACHIEVED THIS MONTH!

Goals: Checklist

	☐
	☐
	☐
	☐
	☐
	☐
	☐
	☐

December
2022

S	M	T	W	T	F	S
				1	2	3
4	5	6	7	8	9	10
11	12	13	14	15	16	17
18	19	20	21	22	23	24
25	26	27	28	29	30	31

Weekly Schedule Planner

Week No. _____

THIS WEEK'S GOALS

TO-DO CHECKLIST

NOTES/REMINDERS

"THE SPEED OF YOUR SUCCESS IS LIMITED ONLY BY YOUR DEDICATION AND WHAT YOU'RE WILLING TO SACRIFICE."

HABIT TRACKER

Week: _____

ACTIVITIES	M	T	W	T	F	S	S

NOTES

Weekly Schedule Planner

Week No. _____

THIS WEEK'S GOALS

TO-DO CHECKLIST

NOTES/REMINDERS

"A FOOL AND HIS MONEY ARE SOON PARTED."

HABIT TRACKER

Week: _____

ACTIVITIES	M	T	W	T	F	S	S

NOTES

Weekly Schedule Planner

Week No. _____

THIS WEEK'S GOALS

TO-DO CHECKLIST

NOTES/REMINDERS

"A BUDGET IS MORE THAN JUST A SERIES OF NUMBERS ON A PAGE; IT IS AN EMBODIMENT OF OUR VALUES."

HABIT TRACKER

Week: _____

ACTIVITIES	M	T	W	T	F	S	S

NOTES

Weekly Schedule Planner

Week No. _____

THIS WEEK'S GOALS

TO-DO CHECKLIST

NOTES/REMINDERS

"BUDGETS ARE BLUEPRINTS AND PRIORITIES."

HABIT TRACKER

Week: _____

ACTIVITIES	M	T	W	T	F	S	S

NOTES

MONTHLY BUDGET

Month :

ITEM	BUDGET	SPENT	REMAINS

TOTAL:

Notes

GIFT PLANNING

DATE:

GIFTS TO BE GIVEN	BUDGET	ACTUAL	
			☑
			☐
			☐
			☐
			☐
			☐
			☐
			☐
			☐

NOTES:

MY TRAVEL PLAN

Date: _____

Date:

Location:

Budget:

Travel To-do List

-
-
-
-
-
-
-

Today's Expenses

Today's Log

- 6 AM
- 7 AM
- 8 AM
- 9 AM
- 10 AM
- 11 AM
- 12 PM
- 1 PM
- 2 PM
- 3 PM
- 4 PM
- 5 PM
- 6 PM
- 7 PM
- 8 PM

Quick Note:

GOALS ACHIEVED THIS MONTH!

Goals: Checklist

- [ ]
- [ ]
- [ ]
- [ ]
- [ ]
- [ ]
- [ ]
- [ ]

YEARLY BUDGET

MONTH	INCOME	SPENT	SAVINGS

NOTES:

www.ingramcontent.com/pod-product-compliance
Lightning Source LLC
Chambersburg PA
CBHW081414080526
44589CB00016B/2530